39102000033638
9/14/2006
Graham, Anna.
Deadly creatures /

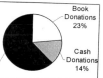

DEADLY
CREATURES

by **Anna Graham**

Consultant: Alison Howard

BEARPORT
PUBLISHING COMPANY, INC.
New York, New York

Picture credits (t=top; b=bottom; c=center; l=left; r=right): Corbis: 6-7 all, 8-9 all. FLPA: 10-11 all, 12-13 all, 20-21 all, 22c, 24-25 all. Natural History Photo Library: 14-15 all, 16-17 all, 18-19 all, 23b, 26-27 all.

Every effort has been made to trace the copyright holders, and we apologize in advance for any unintentional omissions. We would be pleased to insert the appropriate acknowledgments in any subsequent edition of this publication.

Library of Congress Cataloging-in-Publication Data
Graham, Anna.
 Deadly creatures / by Anna Graham.
    p. cm. — (Top 10s)
 Includes index.
 ISBN 1-59716-064-4 (lib. bdg.) — ISBN 1-59716-101-2 (pbk.)
 1. Poisonous animals—Juvenile literature. 2. Dangerous animals—Juvenile literature. I. Title. II. Series.

QL100.G73 2006
591.6'5—dc22

                                         2005010285

For more information, write to Bearport Publishing Company, Inc., 101 Fifth Avenue, Suite 6R, New York, New York 10003. Printed in the United States of America.

            1 2 3 4 5 6 7 8 9 10

CONTENTS

INTRODUCTION

This book describes the world's most deadly creatures. Many animals can hurt people. However, the creatures in this book are different. These animals are killers. Our Top 10 deadly creatures were rated on a scale from one to ten in the following categories:

SHAPE

Animals with the most complex shapes were given the most points. A complicated shape can make a creature hard to recognize and avoid. Its shape may also help the creature attack its victims.

DANGER

Here we looked at all the body features that make an animal dangerous. We also considered whether the animal is aggressive, how many places it's found, and whether it is common or rare. The score is a combination of all these factors.

NO. 9 — SYDNEY FUNNEL-WEB SPIDER

The funnel-web spider lives in and around Sydney, Australia. It is probably the most dangerous spider on Earth. Though it lives mostly in the forest, the Sydney funnel-web spider is often found in garages, backyards, and even under the floors of houses.

SHAPE
The Sydney funnel web is very large for a spider. Its body is about 1–2 inches (3–5 cm) long.

The Sydney funnel-web spider injects its venom through a pair of sharp, curved fangs.

DANGER
Most spiders have venom that is too weak to hurt large animals. The Sydney funnel-web spider is different: its venom is very deadly to humans. Also, its jaws can bite through clothing.

ATTACK
This spider is an active hunter. When threatened, it raises its head and front legs before delivering its deadly bite.

ATTACK

4/10

Looking at the way an animal attacks and kills its victims is important. Animals that have an unusual way of attacking got higher scores than those that use the same methods as other creatures. Points were also added to the scores of animals that take their victims by surprise.

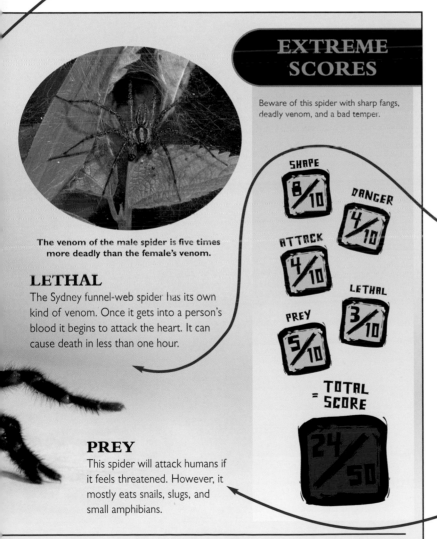

EXTREME SCORES

Beware of this spider with sharp fangs, deadly venom, and a bad temper.

The venom of the male spider is five times more deadly than the female's venom.

SHAPE 8/10

DANGER 4/10

ATTACK 4/10

PREY 5/10

LETHAL 3/10

= **TOTAL SCORE** 24/50

LETHAL
The Sydney funnel-web spider has its own kind of venom. Once it gets into a person's blood it begins to attack the heart. It can cause death in less than one hour.

PREY
This spider will attack humans if it feels threatened. However, it mostly eats snails, slugs, and small amphibians.

LETHAL

3/10

In this category our only concern was with the physical effects of the **venom**, **toxin**, or other things that cause death.

PREY

5/10

Here we focused on what these creatures eat. We looked at the size and type of **prey**. We also considered whether the prey was easy or difficult to find.

9

Most people think that frogs are harmless. However, the poison dart frog will change their minds. This poisonous frog lives in the tropical **rain forests** of Central and South America. Hunters sometimes smear the frog's poison on the tips of their arrows and pipe darts.

SHAPE

The poison dart frog is about 1–2 inches (3–5 cm) long and has brightly colored skin.

DANGER

This small **amphibian** uses poison to defend itself. The bright colors warn **predators** that these frogs are not good to eat.

ATTACK

A thin layer of deadly slime covers the poison dart frog. The slime oozes from small **glands** in the frog's skin.

The frog's bright color is a warning: Do not touch!

The poison dart frog is small, beautiful, and deadly. If you see one, do not touch it.

LETHAL

The frog's glands make a poison that stops its victim's muscles from working and causes death. Just touching a poison dart frog can kill an adult human.

PREY

This deadly frog mainly feeds on insects, especially ants. It needs to eat ants in order to make its poison.

The skin of the poison dart frog is covered with poisonous slime.

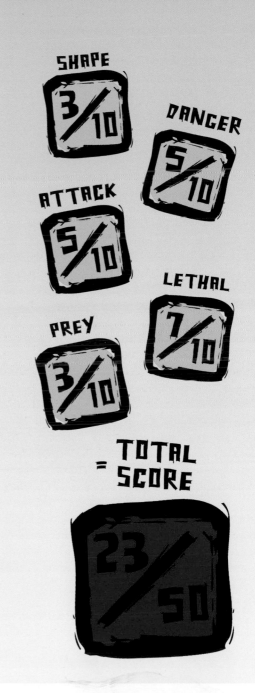

SHAPE 3/10

DANGER 5/10

ATTACK 5/10

LETHAL 7/10

PREY 3/10

= TOTAL SCORE

23/50

SYDNEY FUNNEL-WEB SPIDER

The funnel-web spider lives in and around Sydney, Australia. It is probably the most dangerous spider on Earth. Though it lives mostly in the forest, the Sydney funnel-web spider is often found in garages, backyards, and even under the floors of houses.

SHAPE

The Sydney funnel-web is very large for a spider. Its body is about 1–2 inches (3–5 cm) long.

The Sydney funnel-web spider injects its venom through a pair of sharp, curved fangs.

DANGER

Most spiders have venom that is too weak to hurt large animals. The Sydney funnel-web spider is different: its venom is very deadly to humans. Also, its jaws can bite through clothing.

ATTACK

This spider is an active hunter. When threatened, it raises its head and front legs before delivering its deadly bite.

The venom of the male spider is five times more deadly than the female's venom.

LETHAL

The Sydney funnel-web spider has its own kind of venom. Once it gets into a person's blood it begins to attack the heart. It can cause death in less than one hour.

PREY

This spider will attack humans if it feels threatened. However, it mostly eats snails, slugs, and small amphibians.

Beware of this spider with sharp fangs, deadly venom, and a bad temper.

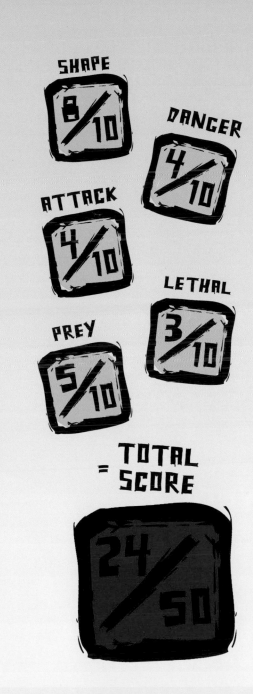

SHAPE
8/10

DANGER
4/10

ATTACK
4/10

LETHAL
3/10

PREY
5/10

= TOTAL SCORE

24/50

The blue-ringed octopus is one of the most beautiful of all sea creatures. It is also one of the most deadly. This small, shy animal lives around **coral reefs** in the Indian and Pacific Oceans. Swimmers and divers have learned not to get near this octopus because it has a very mean bite.

SHAPE

The body of the blue-ringed octopus is only about 4 inches (10 cm) long. Eight **tentacles** surround its mouth.

DANGER

The blue-ringed octopus is the only octopus with a venomous bite. People swimming in the sea who disturb this octopus are likely to get bitten.

ATTACK

This octopus has a sharp beak that can slice flesh. Its venomous **saliva** then flows into the wound.

A blue-ringed octopus
weighs about one ounce (28 g).

LETHAL

At first the octopus's bite feels like a bee sting. Then the victim goes numb and dies. There is no known cure for blue-ringed octopus venom.

PREY

The octopus mainly eats crabs and wounded fish that cannot swim away quickly.

The blue rings only appear when the octopus is angry or frightened. In either case, it may bite.

The blue-ringed octopus is a beautiful but deadly animal. It is very active during the day when most people go swimming. Be careful!

SHAPE 6/10

DANGER 5/10

ATTACK 6/10

LETHAL 5/10

PREY 6/10

= TOTAL SCORE

28/50

STONEFISH

Meet the fish that looks just like a rock: the stonefish. It lives around the coasts of the Indian and Pacific Oceans. Not only is the stonefish very ugly, it is also very dangerous. In fact, the stonefish is the most poisonous fish in the sea. Its sharp spines can easily go through flesh and inject deadly venom.

SHAPE

The stonefish can grow up to 24 inches (61 cm) long. Its lumpy skin helps hide its shape.

DANGER

The stonefish likes to lie half buried on the ocean floor, waiting to attack its prey.

A stonefish does not swim away when disturbed. It turns to face the intruder.

ATTACK

There are 13 sharp spines in the fin that runs along the stonefish's back. Each spine can inject a deadly dose of venom.

LETHAL

If you step on a stonefish, you will start to hurt right away. The pain will quickly get worse. Some victims die within a few hours.

PREY

The stonefish only uses its spines for defense. It catches shrimp and small fish in its mouth.

Each spine along the stonefish's back contains nasty surprises.

The stonefish's spines are filled with deadly venom. Make sure that the next stone you step on is really a stone.

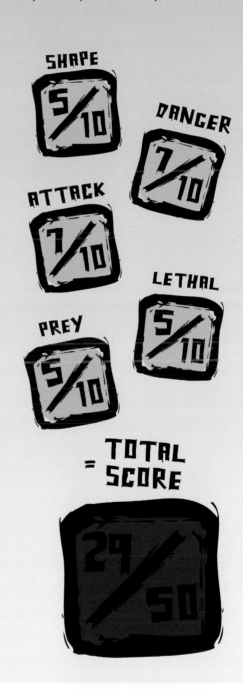

SHAPE 5/10

DANGER 7/10

ATTACK 7/10

LETHAL 5/10

PREY 5/10

= TOTAL SCORE

29/50

PALESTINE SCORPION

The Palestine scorpion is the most dangerous scorpion in the world. It is found in and around the **deserts** of the Middle East and North Africa.

SHAPE

The Palestine scorpion is about 3–4 inches (8–10 cm) long. It has two large **pincers** and a deadly **stinger** at the end of its tail.

DANGER

The Palestine scorpion often hides under rocks or around loose sand and stones. If disturbed, it will lash out with its deadly tail. Children are often stung while playing or walking.

ATTACK

The scorpion's sharp stinger goes through flesh and injects its deadly venom. The Palestine scorpion will sometimes sting a victim over and over again.

The stinger at the end of the curving tail carries deadly venom.

The scorpion's yellow color
helps it hide in desert sand.

The Palestine scorpion is so deadly
that it lives up to its nickname —
"death stalker."

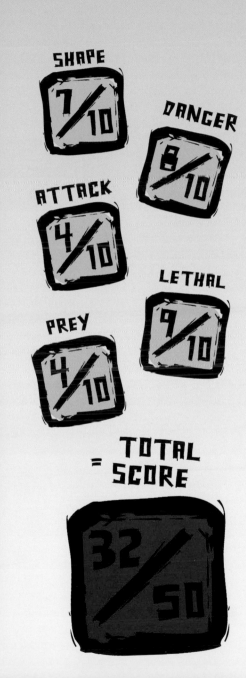

SHAPE
7/10

DANGER
8/10

ATTACK
4/10

LETHAL
9/10

PREY
4/10

= TOTAL SCORE
32/50

LETHAL
One drop of the
Palestine scorpion's
venom is enough to
kill an animal much
larger than itself. Luckily,
scientists have developed an
antidote for this scorpion's sting.

PREY
When the Palestine scorpion
hunts, it doesn't use its stinger to kill. Instead,
it tears its prey apart with its pincers.
The stinger is only
used if the hunt
turns into a fight.

FIERCE SNAKE

The fierce snake is not as famous as the cobra or rattlesnake. However, its venom is a lot more deadly. Luckily, the fierce snake is only found in northern Australia where it is very rare.

SHAPE

The fierce snake has a slim, smooth body. It can grow up to 8 feet (2 m) long.

The fierce snake has the deadliest venom of any snake.

DANGER

The fierce snake is usually shy. If you are unlucky enough to see one, however, walk slowly away. It can be very mean if disturbed.

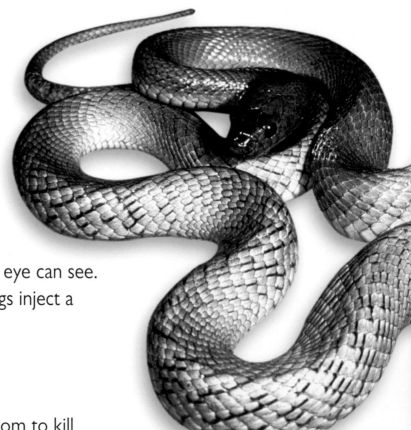

ATTACK

This snake can strike faster than the eye can see. As it bites its victim, two hollow fangs inject a small dose of its venom.

LETHAL

The fierce snake carries enough venom to kill about 250,000 mice.

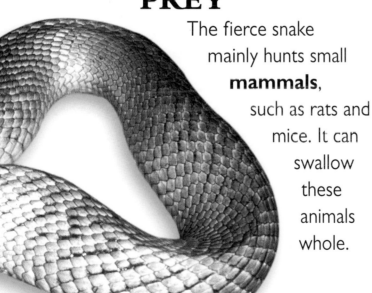

Inside the snake's mouth are two sharp fangs that inject venom.

PREY

The fierce snake mainly hunts small **mammals**, such as rats and mice. It can swallow these animals whole.

The fierce snake is deadly, but it is also very rare.

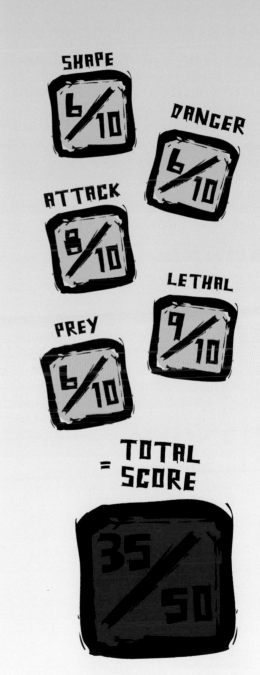

SHAPE
6/10

DANGER
6/10

ATTACK
8/10

LETHAL
9/10

PREY
6/10

= TOTAL SCORE

35/50

This small insect has probably caused more human deaths than any other animal—and all of them by accident. The female Anopheles mosquito just wants to drink a little human blood. However, while she drinks our blood, she can also give us a deadly disease called **malaria**.

SHAPE

The Anopheles mosquito has six legs and a single pair of wings.

DANGER

A tiny **microbe** often lives in the Anopheles mosquito's body. When the mosquito sucks blood, the microbe leaks into the victim's blood. In humans, this microbe causes malaria, which is sometimes fatal—especially in children.

ATTACK

This mosquito does not bite with teeth. She has a feeding tube like a hollow needle. She pokes this tube into human skin to suck up blood.

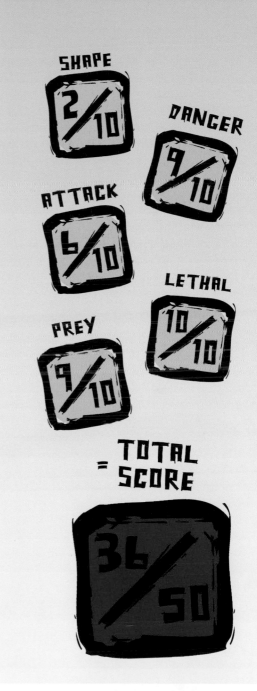

Female mosquitoes must drink
blood in order to lay eggs.

LETHAL

Taking a tiny amount of blood from humans is
not harmful. However, giving people malaria is
deadly. The disease kills
almost 3 million people
every year.

**Each mosquito takes
just a tiny drop of blood.**

PREY

Mosquitoes are only interested in drinking the
blood of mammals. Humans are easy targets.

Small and hard to see, the Anopheles
does not look like a killer. However, it
has caused millions of human deaths.

SHAPE
2/10

DANGER
9/10

ATTACK
6/10

LETHAL
10/10

PREY
9/10

= TOTAL SCORE

36/50

The beaked sea snake makes about half of all sea-snake attacks. It's also responsible for 90 percent of deaths from sea-snake bites. Its venom is deadlier than most land snakes.

SHAPE

The back half of a sea snake is flattened to help it swim.

DANGER

The beaked sea snake often gets caught in fishing nets, which makes it very angry. People trying to take the snakes out of the nets often get bitten.

ATTACK

Sea snakes have much shorter fangs than land snakes. These fangs, however, are just as sharp and deadly. The venom of a beaked sea snake acts very quickly.

The beaked sea snake grows to about 4 feet (1 m) long.

Bright black markings make this deadly sea snake easy to identify.

LETHAL

This creature has the sixth most deadly snake venom in the world. The venom attacks the victim's muscles, which causes the victim to stop breathing. Death quickly follows.

PREY

The beaked sea snake can swallow fish that are up to twice its own size.

This bad-tempered animal has sharp fangs and deadly venom. The beaked sea snake would certainly not make a good pet.

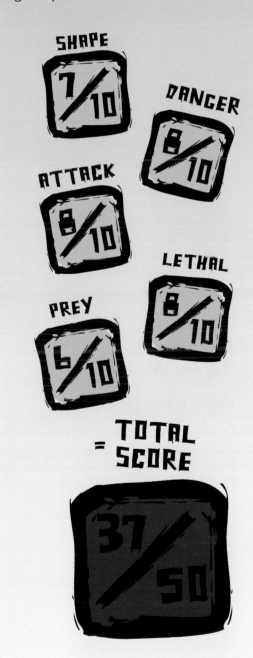

SHAPE
7/10

DANGER
8/10

ATTACK
8/10

LETHAL
8/10

PREY
6/10

= TOTAL SCORE
37/50

PIRANHA

This fish has earned its nickname the "wolf of the waters." Piranhas have sharp teeth and hunt in groups. One piranha will give you a nasty bite. A group of them will strip all the flesh from your bones. The piranha is found in the Amazon and other rivers in South America.

SHAPE

The average length of a piranha is about 12 inches (30 cm). However, a well-fed piranha can reach twice that size.

DANGER

The piranha has a superb sense of smell. It can detect blood in the water from more than a mile away. It lives in **shoals** of up to 100 fish. These fish can all attack at the same time.

ATTACK

Piranhas don't kill their prey first. They just start eating it alive. Their teeth are razor sharp. When they have finished feeding, only their victim's bones are left.

When piranhas are in a feeding frenzy, the water seems to churn and turns red with blood.

The teeth of a piranha can slice through flesh.

LETHAL

Piranhas will attack anything—even humans. Most victims die from loss of blood.

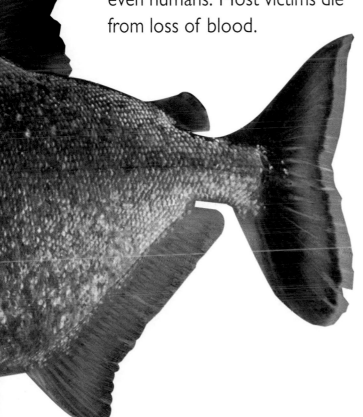

PREY

The piranha normally eats fish, crabs, and small mammals.

The flesh-eating piranha is a good reason to stay out of the water in certain places. This fish will start eating swimmers without giving any warning.

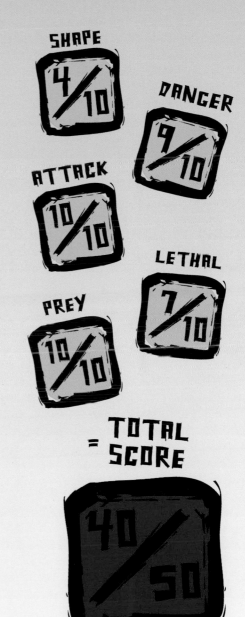

SHAPE
4/10

DANGER
9/10

ATTACK
10/10

LETHAL
7/10

PREY
10/10

= TOTAL SCORE
40/50

No living creature is more deadly than the sea wasp. This small, boneless jellyfish is found in the seas around Australia. It has dozens of stinging tentacles. Each tentacle is filled with deadly venom that kills almost instantly. To make matters worse, the clear and colorless sea wasp is almost impossible to see underwater.

SHAPE

The sea wasp has a four-sided shape (it is also known as the box jelly). It grows to about 12 inches (30 cm) wide. Its tentacles are more than 39 inches (99 cm) long.

DANGER

Sea wasps sting hundreds of people every year. Many of their victims die. To protect people, some beaches in Australia are closed when there are sea wasps around.

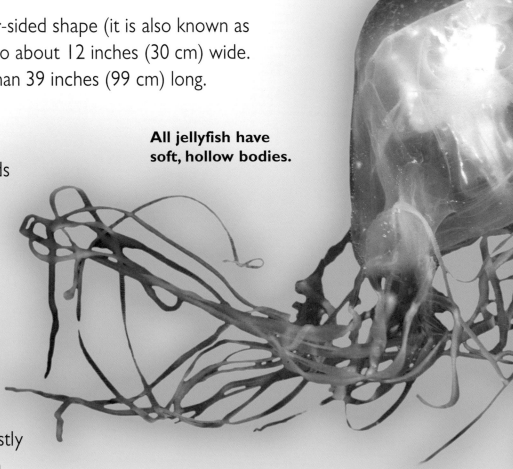

All jellyfish have soft, hollow bodies.

PREY

The sea wasp feeds mostly on shrimp and small fish.

The white blobs on the tentacles are clusters of tiny, spring-loaded stingers.

ATTACK

Every sea-wasp tentacle has thousands of tiny stingers with sharp points. These stingers are set off by the slightest touch. They then inject deadly venom into the victim.

LETHAL

Sea-wasp victims feel a sudden burning pain. The venom may stop a person's heartbeat within minutes. A single sea wasp carries enough venom to kill about 50 people.

Sea wasps are nearly invisible killers armed with deadly, fast-acting venom. Sometimes there are thousands and thousands of them in just a small part of the sea.

SHAPE 10/10

DANGER 10/10

ATTACK 6/10

LETHAL 8/10

PREY 7/10

= TOTAL SCORE

41/50

CLOSE
BUT NOT CLOSE ENOUGH

Before deciding our Top 10 deadly creatures, we also considered these animals. They are all deadly killers, but not quite deadly enough to make the Top 10.

CONE SHELL

The cone shell is a kind of sea snail. Its shell is about 3–4 inches (8–10 cm) long. It is often brightly colored. If you saw one on a beach, you might be tempted to pick it up. Don't! All cone shells can give a painful sting. Some **species** can also inject a deadly toxin.

GILA MONSTER

This strange-looking **reptile** is one of only two venomous lizards in the whole world. It lives in both the deserts of the southwestern United States and northern Mexico. The Gila monster has short teeth. Each tooth can inject venom that is strong enough to kill an adult human.

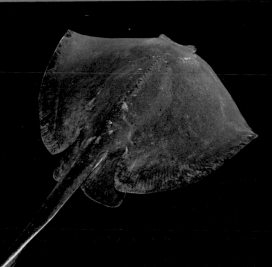

STINGRAY

Stingrays are closely related to sharks. However, you don't have to worry about their bite. It's the venomous stinger in their tails that's the problem. This fish likes shallow water and often hides in the sand on the ocean floor. Swimmers beware!

HARVESTER ANT

Harvester ants are common in the United States. They like to collect plant seeds. If humans get in their way, the ants may sting them with a dangerous venom. This poison causes pain, itching, and sometimes death.

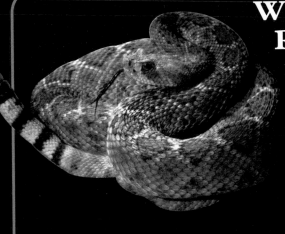

WESTERN DIAMONDBACK RATTLESNAKE

The western diamondback is the strongest and most fierce North American rattlesnake. This dangerous snake can use its venom on prey that is small enough to swallow. Larger animals are warned by the sound of a rattle. They better beware—this killer bites fast and deep.

STATS

NO. 10 POISON DART FROG

Extreme Scores

Shape	3
Danger	5
Attack	5
Lethal	7
Prey	3

TOTAL SCORE
23/50

NO. 9 SYDNEY FUNNEL-WEB SPIDER

Extreme Scores

Shape	8
Danger	4
Attack	4
Lethal	3
Prey	5

TOTAL SCORE
24/50

NO. 8 BLUE-RINGED OCTOPUS

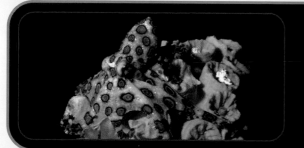

Extreme Scores

Shape	6
Danger	5
Attack	6
Lethal	5
Prey	6

TOTAL SCORE
28/50

NO. 7 STONEFISH

Extreme Scores

Shape	5
Danger	7
Attack	7
Lethal	5
Prey	5

TOTAL SCORE
29/50

NO. 6 PALESTINE SCORPION

Extreme Scores

Shape	7
Danger	8
Attack	4
Lethal	9
Prey	4

TOTAL SCORE
32/50

NO. 5 FIERCE SNAKE

Extreme Scores

Shape	6
Danger	6
Attack	8
Lethal	9
Prey	6

TOTAL SCORE 35 / 50

NO. 4 ANOPHELES MOSQUITO

Extreme Scores

Shape	2
Danger	9
Attack	6
Lethal	10
Prey	9

TOTAL SCORE 36 / 50

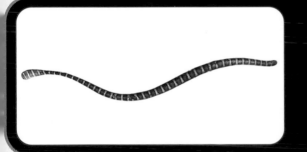

NO. 3 BEAKED SEA SNAKE

Extreme Scores

Shape	7
Danger	8
Attack	8
Lethal	8
Prey	6

TOTAL SCORE 37 / 50

NO. 2 PIRANHA

Extreme Scores

Shape	4
Danger	9
Attack	10
Lethal	7
Prey	10

TOTAL SCORE 40 / 50

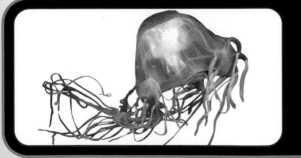

NO. 1 SEA WASP

Extreme Scores

Shape	10
Danger	10
Attack	6
Lethal	8
Prey	7

TOTAL SCORE 41 / 50

GLOSSARY

amphibian (am-FIB-ee-uhn) an animal that lives part of its life in water and part on land

antidote (AN-ti-dote) a remedy used to stop the effects of a poison

coral reefs (KOR-uhl REEFS) a group of coral, which is made up of the skeletons of tiny creatures, found near the surface of the water

deserts (DEZ-urts) areas of land with little or no water and vegetation

glands (GLANDS) body organs that secrete chemicals

malaria (muh-LAIR-ee-uh) a disease, transmitted to humans by the bite of an infected female Anopheles mosquito, that causes chills, fever, sweating, and even death

mammals (MAM-uhlz) animals that are warm-blooded, nurse their young with milk, and have hair or fur on their skin

microbe (MYE-krobe) an extremely small living thing that can cause disease

pincers (PIN-surs) the front claws of a lobster, crab, scorpion, or similar creature

predators (PRED-uh-turz) animals that hunt other animals for food

prey (PRAY) an animal that is hunted or caught for food

rain forests (RAYN FOR-ists) a dense tropical forest with a yearly rainfall of 100 inches (254 cm)

reptile (REP-tile) a cold-blooded animal that has dry, scaly skin, and uses lungs to breathe

saliva (suh-LYE-vah) clear watery liquid found in the mouths of humans and animals

shoals (SHOLES) a large group of fish or other marine animals

species (SPEE-sheez) groups that animals or plants are divided into according to similar characteristics

stinger (STING-ur) a sharp part of an animal that is used to sting

tentacles (TEN-tuh-kuhls) long flexible limbs on some animals used for feeling or grasping

toxin (TOX-in) a poison produced by certain animals that can cause sickness or death if it's injected into another animal or person

venom (VEN-uhm) a poison from an animal, such as a snake, spider, or scorpion, usually transmitted by a bite or sting

INDEX